I  ing

Fossil Hunter

by Leonie Bennett

Consultant: Dougal Dixon

CONTENTS

Words in **bold** are explained in the glossary.

Finding out about dinosaurs

Dinosaurs lived a long time ago.

There were many different kinds of dinosaur.

Eoraptor was one of the first dinosaurs.

Eoraptor
ee-o-rap-tor

These men try to find out about dinosaurs. It is their job. They are fossil hunters.

Fossil hunters

Dinosaur fossils

We learn about dinosaurs by looking at **fossils**.

Fossils are rocks shaped like dead animals' bones. It takes thousands of years for fossils to form.

This is the fossil of a dinosaur **skull**.

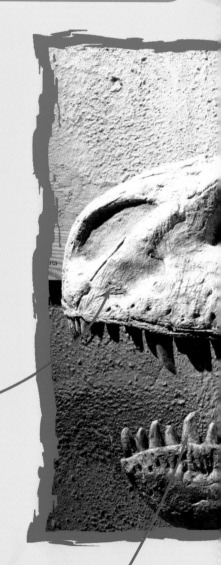

Sharp teeth

Big eyes

Strong jaws

This dinosaur had sharp teeth. We can tell it was a scary hunter.

7

What do fossil hunters do?

This is Simon. It is his job to look for fossils.

Simon looks for fossils in rocks.

He digs the fossils out of the rock very carefully.

Rock

Hammer

Where does Simon look for fossils?

Fossils are found in many places.

Some are found on the beach.

Beach

Some are found in rocky mountains.

Mountains

Fossils have been found all over the world.

Simon finds a fossil

When Simon finds a fossil, he uses a brush to clean it.

Brush

Fossil

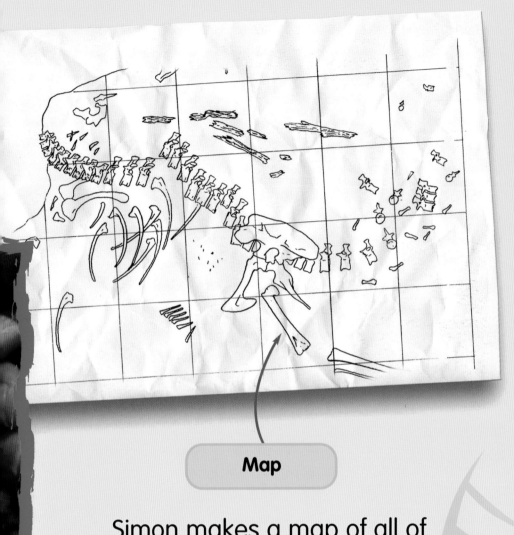

Map

Simon makes a map of all of the fossils he finds.

He writes down what it is and where he found it.

What tools does Simon use?

Simon uses a hammer
to get the fossils out
of the rock.

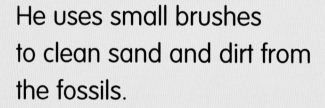

He uses small brushes
to clean sand and dirt from
the fossils.

Fossil hunters also use computers to find out about dinosaurs.

Studying a footprint

Simon can tell a lot from this footprint.

Dinosaur footprint

The dinosaur that made it was very big. It walked on three toes.

Simon thinks it was an Iguanodon.

Iguanodon ate plants. It was about ten metres long.

Iguanodon
ig-wan-o-don

Three toes

Studying a skull

Simon found this dinosaur skull.
It is very big!

The dinosaur had big
sharp teeth.

Teeth

18

Simon thinks it was
a T. rex.

What happens to the fossils?

Most fossils go to museums.

The museums put the fossils together.

Apatosaurus skeleton

The museum tells us about the dinosaur.

Now everybody can find out more about dinosaurs!

Glossary

fossil
A part of an animal or plant that has turned into stone. Footprints can also be fossils.

fossil hunters
Scientists whose job it is to find fossils.

museum

A place where rare or interesting things are put on display.

skull

The bones in the head.

T. rex

The short name for Tyrannosaurus rex – a fierce meat-eating dinosaur.

Index

Copyright © ticktock Entertainment Ltd 2008
First published in Great Britain in 2008 by ticktock Media Ltd.,
Unit 2, Orchard Business Centre, North Farm Road, Tunbridge Wells, Kent TN2 3XF
ISBN 978 1 84696 767 2 pbk
Printed in China

We would like to thank: Penny Worms, Shirley Bickler, Suzanne Baker and the National Literacy Trust.

Picture credits (t=top, b=bottom, c=centre, l-left, r=right, OFC= outside front cover)
Lisa Alderson: 4; Robin Carter: 13; Corbis: 5, 8-9, 18b, 22b; Luis Rey: 17, 19; Shutterstock: 1, 7, 10, 11, 12, 14b & t, 15, 16, 18t, 20-21, 21t, 22c, 23b, 22t, 23t.

Every effort has been made to trace the copyright holders, and we apologise in advance for any unintentional omissions. We would be pleased to insert the appropriate acknowledgements in any subsequent edition of this publication.